Pope John Paul II

by Jill C. Wheeler

Breaking Barriers

visit us at
www.abdopub.com

Published by ABDO & Daughters, an imprint of ABDO
Publishing Company, 4940 Viking Drive, Suite 622, Edina,
Minnesota 55435. Copyright ©2003 by Abdo Consulting
Group, Inc. International copyrights reserved in all countries.
No part of this book may be reproduced in any form without
written permission from the publisher.

Printed in the United States.

Edited by Paul Joseph
Graphic Design: John Hamilton
Cover Design: Mighty Media
Interior Photos: AP/Photo, p. 5, 23
Corbis, p. 1, 6, 9, 10, 13, 18, 21, 25, 26, 29, 31, 33, 35, 37, 39,
41, 43, 44, 47, 48, 50, 51, 53, 55, 57, 59, 60, 61
Digital Stock, p. 15, 16

Library of Congress Cataloging-in-Publication Data

Wheeler, Jill C., 1964-
    Pope John Paul II / Jill C. Wheeler.
        p. cm. — (Breaking barriers)
    Includes index.
    Summary: Traces the life of Karol Wojtyla from his childhood and
student years in Poland through his ordination as a priest, his election
as Pope John Paul II, and his efforts to strengthen the Catholic
Church.
        ISBN 1-57765-740-3
        1. John Paul II, Pope, 1920- —Juvenile literature. 2. Popes—
Biography—Juvenile literature. [1. John Paul II, Pope, 1920- 2.
Popes.] I. Title.

BX1378.5. W48 2002
282'.092—dc21
[B]

                                                2001046374

Contents

Breaking New Ground

*M*any scholars believe Damascus, Syria, is the world's oldest city. Umayyad (oo-MY-ad) Mosque in Damascus is the world's oldest surviving stone mosque. It was built between A.D. 705 and 715. Umayyad Mosque is one of the greatest treasures of Islamic art. Many years ago, a Christian church stood where the mosque stands now. Today, Muslims go to the Umayyad Mosque to pray.

On May 6, 2001, a special man visited the mosque. Like the other visitors, he carefully removed his shoes before stepping inside. Unlike most visitors, however, he came with a crowd of spectators who cheered as he entered the mosque. Afterward, he spoke to Muslims and Christians alike. He asked them to forgive each other and seek forgiveness from God. He also urged them to work toward understanding each other.

The visitor was Pope John Paul II, the first pope ever to set foot in a mosque. The history-making visit was just one in a long line of groundbreaking events for Pope John Paul II.

Pope John Paul II

Pope John Paul II

Pope John Paul II has been called the most recognized person in the world. As pope, he is the leader of the Roman Catholic Church, a religious group that has approximately one billion believers worldwide. He is the most traveled pope in history, with more than 500,000 miles (804,500 km) logged. He has visited more than 115 countries, and he speaks eight languages fluently.

Many people have criticized Pope John Paul II's conservative beliefs. Catholics are supposed to believe that the pope's word on matters of faith and morals is infallible, but many people disagree with him. They believe his views on birth control, abortion, homosexuality, and women in the priesthood are too conservative. Many people think he has not helped the Catholic Church adapt to the modern world.

Yet even Pope John Paul II's critics may agree that he is uniquely gifted. "This is not a pope who looks at the public opinion polls," said writer Father Thomas Reese. "He says what he thinks is right and wrong from conviction. And that's why people admire him. He's a man of integrity and prayer, even if they don't agree with him."

Little Lolek

*P*ope John Paul II was born Karol Jozef Wojtyla (voy-TIH-wah) on May 18, 1920, in Wadowice, Poland. Wadowice was a small, working-class community near the Polish city of Krakow.

Karol's parents were Emilia and Karol Wojtyla. Karol Sr. was a lieutenant in the Polish army. Emilia was a schoolteacher before she married Karol Sr. The Wojtylas called their young son Lolek, a common nickname for Karol. Lolek had a brother named Edmund. He was 15 years older than Lolek. Lolek also had an older sister, but she died while still a baby.

The Wojtyla family never had much money. They lived in a modest, three-room apartment across the street from their church, the Church of Our Lady.

Like most Poles, the Wojtylas were Catholics. Church was an important part of their lives. For young Lolek, it was no different. He prayed with his family and attended Mass on Sundays. When he got older, Lolek became an altar boy. Sometimes Lolek and his friends pretended they were priests. They dressed up in robes and played in front of a pretend altar in the living room. Lolek's mother told friends that little Lolek would grow up to be a great man, a priest.

*Karol Wojtyla
and his mother.*

Karol Wojtyla as an altar boy.

Lolek's mother was often sick. In April 1929,
when Lolek was just eight years old, his mother died
from problems with her heart and kidneys. Three and
a half years later, tragedy struck again. Lolek's brother
Edmund, a doctor, was treating a patient with scarlet
fever. Edmund caught the disease and died. Now the
Wojtyla family was only Lolek and his father.

Lolek and his father had always been close. The recent deaths in their family brought the two even closer. Lolek noticed that his father became even more religious after his mother's death. "Sometimes I would wake up during the night and find my father on his knees, just as I would always see him kneeling in the parish church," he remembered. "His example was in a way my first seminary, a kind of domestic seminary."

Karol Sr. had retired from the Polish army shortly before Emilia died. So he had time to devote to Lolek, doing all the sewing, washing, and cooking for him. Karol Sr. used his army experience in his home life. He had Lolek follow a strict schedule of Mass, school, and homework. Lolek had only a little free time each day to play soccer or swim with friends in the local river. Lolek usually came home at noon to have lunch with his father.

Living under his father's strict rules, Lolek flourished. He was popular among classmates. His teachers recalled him being an outstanding student. Lolek enjoyed reading Polish literature, and he also played sports. He became one of his school's best soccer players. He played goalie for the team. He also liked spending time in the nearby Tatra Mountains, where he became an excellent skier and hiker.

In the early 1930s, Lolek became interested in theater. He loved it from the start. In high school, Lolek took part in the drama club. He acted in and produced plays. Lolek learned difficult Polish folk dances. His voice grew into a rich baritone, and he discovered he had a natural speaking ability.

Lolek's speaking skills earned him a special honor just before he graduated from high school. Bishop Adam Stefan Sapieha of Krakow planned to visit Lolek's school. Lolek was chosen to speak to Sapieha on behalf of the students. After the speech, Sapieha asked one of Lolek's teachers if the young man planned to become a priest. The teacher replied, "Doesn't look like it at the moment." The bishop answered, "Pity. He'd make a fine one."

As Lolek graduated in 1938, he had his mind set on a career in theater. He wanted to study at Krakow's esteemed Jagiellonian (ya-gel-LO-nee-uhn) University. Poland's King Casmir III the Great founded the school in 1364, making it the second-oldest university in central Europe. The university attracted science and philosophy students from throughout the continent.

Before Lolek began classes, he spent the summer in a youth army. It was part of the military training required of young men in Poland during the 1930s. Lolek's outfit built roads in the mountains south of Wadowice. While in the youth army, Lolek also served at Mass.

In the fall, Lolek and his father moved to Krakow to be near the university. They moved into a basement apartment. Lolek soon began his studies in Polish language and literature at Jagiellonian University. He also joined the student drama group and performed in plays.

Life for Lolek and his father was going smoothly. In 1939, however, things began to change. Adolf Hitler, Germany's ruler, was making plans to take over Poland, and those plans would change Lolek's life forever.

Karol Wojtyla (fourth from left, seated) at school. The man sitting second from left is his father.

A Nation Under Siege

*W*ojtyla spent the summer of 1939 at the required military training. When he returned to the university that fall, he looked forward to another year of studying literature and drama. His plans were ruined on September 1, 1939, when Hitler's troops attacked Poland.

Hitler's army used a quick, violent attack method called *blitzkrieg*. His army invaded so quickly and with such force that the Polish army could not defend itself. It did not have the advanced equipment that the German army had. Often, Poles fought on horseback while Germans fought with tanks. Poland was forced to surrender to Germany a month later.

Hitler promptly made Poland into a slave state to serve his army. He used his secret police, called the *Gestapo*, to round up the Polish leaders, teachers, and priests. Hitler believed that if the educated leaders were gone, the Polish people would remain obedient to the Germans. Hitler wanted the Poles to work for him. He did not want the Poles to think for themselves. He and the other Germans who thought this way were called Nazis.

*A German soldier
throws a grenade.*

Starved prisoners at a concentration camp in Ebensee, Austria.

The Nazis captured many of the teachers at Jagiellonian University. Most were sent to concentration camps. Over the course of World War II, more than six million Poles died in these camps. Three million of them were Jews. One of the most horrible and well-known concentration camps, called Auschwitz, was located near Krakow.

Wojtyla was among a group of students that refused to submit to the Nazis. They believed that continuing their education was the best way to fight back for Poland. The students formed a secret university. Their small groups met privately in people's homes to study and hear lessons. Whenever the students met, they risked being caught by the Nazis.

In 1940, Wojtyla attended a church discussion group called the Living Rosary. A layman named Jan Tyranowski led the group. He soon became a spiritual mentor to Wojtyla. Tyranowski introduced Wojtyla to the writings of Saint John of the Cross, a sixteenth-century Spanish priest. These writings made a large impact on Wojtyla's life, and he continued to study them for many years.

Workers blast rock from a quarry with dynamite.

During this time, Wojtyla had to take a job in order to avoid being sent to a labor camp. He and a close friend worked in a limestone quarry owned by a chemical company. Wojtyla's first job was to shovel stones onto railcars after workers had dynamited a section of the quarry wall. He worked in air thick with dust, amid the deafening noise of hammers and drills. The quarry work was backbreaking and dangerous. Once, a worker was killed right beside Wojtyla. Eventually, Wojtyla's job was to help dynamite the quarry walls. Later, he got a job working inside the chemical factory.

What little joy Wojtyla had, came from his secret studies and his activities in an underground drama group, called the Rhapsodic Theater. It put on secret performances that emphasized Polish culture and history. The performances helped the audience remember their heritage and find the strength to continue resisting the Nazis.

One of Hitler's missions was to kill all the Jewish people in Poland. Hitler believed Jews were inferior to others and deserved to die. Wojtyla helped some of his Jewish friends during that time. Like other Poles, he heard rumors of terrible events at Auschwitz. The stories were so horrible that he had a hard time believing them. Sadly, they turned out to be true. The Nazis killed about two million people at Auschwitz.

Suffering was all around Wojtyla. "Sometimes I would ask myself: so many young people of my age are losing their lives, why not me?" he wrote in later years. In February 1941, the suffering hit him directly. He came home after dinner one day to find that his father had died. At age 20, Wojtyla was all alone. He prayed over his father's body all night, trying to deal with his loss.

"After my father's death, I gradually became aware of my true path," Wojtyla recalled. "I was working at the factory and devoting myself... to my taste for literature and drama. My priestly vocation took shape in the midst of all that, like an inner fact of absolute clarity. In the autumn, I knew that I was called..."

Father Wojtyla

*T*he challenge Wojtyla faced now was how to become a priest. The Nazis had made it illegal to study at a seminary. They knew how important the Catholic Church was to the Polish people. To control the Poles, they had to destroy the church.

In October 1942, Wojtyla joined a group of former Jagiellonian University teachers who had formed a secret theology department. Their activities were illegal according to the Nazis' rules. Once again, Wojtyla knew the Nazis would kill him if they learned what he was doing. For 22 months, Wojtyla studied in secret.

During this time, Wojtyla continued working at his job in the chemical factory. One night in February 1944, Wojtyla was walking home from work when a German truck struck him. The driver did not stop to help Wojtyla, who lay unconscious on the side of the road. A passerby found him and got him to the hospital. Wojtyla viewed his recovery as "a time for spiritual retreat, a gift from God."

Pope John Paul II was ordained as a priest in 1946, shortly after World War II.

In August 1944, the Russian army began pushing the Germans out of Poland. The Russians encouraged the Poles to revolt against the Germans, then failed to stand behind them. Thousands of Poles died when the Germans fought back. After the Poles surrendered, Hitler ordered the German army to destroy Poland's capital, Warsaw.

Adam Stefan Sapieha, now the archbishop of Krakow, was afraid that his theology students, including Wojtyla, would be caught up in the bloodshed. To protect the students, Sapieha let them hide in his residence. Wojtyla ate, slept, and studied in the same building. He and the other students did not leave for fear they would be caught and killed.

By January 1945, the Russian army had seized control of Poland from the Germans. The Russians allowed universities to reopen, so Wojtyla was able to finish his studies at Jagiellonian University. During this time, Archbishop Sapieha had become a cardinal. On November 1, 1946, Cardinal Sapieha ordained Wojtyla as a priest of the Roman Catholic Church.

Polish Jews are rounded up by German troops during the Nazi occupation of Warsaw, Poland.

After ordaining Wojtyla, Sapieha decided to send the bright young priest to Rome for further study. Wojtyla spent two years studying at the Angelicum University in Rome. Sapieha had arranged for Wojtyla to live in the Belgian College while he studied. The Belgian College served as a boarding house for students studying in Rome. In the summer, Wojtyla traveled to France, Belgium, and Holland. He learned languages easily. Soon he was speaking fluent Italian, as well as Latin, Polish, and some French. He earned a doctorate degree in philosophy in 1948.

When Wojtyla returned to Poland, the Russian Communist Party controlled the country. The communist government and the Catholic Church had an uneasy relationship. More than 90 percent of the Polish population was Catholic. But the communists outlawed religious education in schools. They censored Catholic newspapers. They sent many priests to prisons or concentration camps.

Wojtyla's first job back in Poland was as an assistant pastor in the rural village of Niegowic. Wojtyla was kind to his parishioners and was always ready to help them. His official duties included celebrating mass, hearing confessions, visiting families, marrying couples, and christening babies. He also taught elementary school in four rural villages.

Monseigneur Adam Stephano Sapieha

A rooftop view of Krakow, Poland.

Wojtyla was at Niegowic for less than a year when the Church transferred him to Saint Florian's Church in Krakow. Wojtyla was glad to be back in Krakow, and he loved working with the people at Saint Florian's Church. He was constantly busy. He visited people, listened to confessions, and even played soccer with the local children. He also worked closely with university students. In between doing his parish duties, Wojtyla enjoyed writing poetry. He had some of his poems published under the pen name Andrzej Jawien.

The people of Saint Florian's Church noticed that Wojtyla always wore an old, patched cassock with no overcoat. They worried he would freeze during the cold Polish winters, so they gave him a new cassock and overcoat. Wojtyla accepted the new cassock, but he gave away the overcoat. He simply didn't want many possessions.

In 1951, Wojtyla was saddened by the death of Cardinal Sapieha. The cardinal had been key in helping Wojtyla get an education in Poland, and later in Rome. Thousands of other Poles were sad to lose their beloved cardinal as well.

Shortly after the cardinal's death, Sapieha's successor spoke with Wojtyla. He told Wojtyla that if he wanted to continue his education, he should take a break from his parish duties and study full time. Wojtyla agreed to the idea. He spent the next two years preparing for an exam that would qualify him to work as an assistant professor. He completed the exam in 1953.

Meanwhile, the communists were making life much more difficult for Poland's Catholic Church. They closed seminaries around the country and sent the students to labor camps. Nearly 1,000 clergy members were imprisoned, including Wojtyla's supervisor.

Wojtyla chose to focus on studying and teaching to avoid being noticed by the communists. First, he taught in secret at the Metropolitan Seminary in Krakow. Later, he taught at the Catholic University of Lublin in eastern Poland. He was a popular teacher at the university. In 1956, he became the head of the university's ethics department.

By this time, relations between the Catholic Church and Poland's communist government were at their worst. Hundreds of bishops and priests were in prison. Fortunately, the leadership in Russia and Poland eventually changed. By 1956, things had slowly improved for the Catholic Church. The government agreed to release some of Poland's imprisoned clergy members. It also allowed schools to resume teaching religious classes for students who chose to attend.

Prisoners at a communist labor camp for boys.

Shaping History

Wojtyla spent the next two years teaching. By this time, his popularity had brought him to the attention of the Catholic leadership. In 1958, Wojtyla was on a canoeing trip when church officials tracked him down. They wanted to appoint him auxiliary bishop of Krakow. Wojtyla accepted the position.

At age 38, Wojtyla was Poland's youngest bishop. He made it a point to visit every parish in his diocese. He challenged himself to meet every priest. He sponsored discussion groups at his home. And he wrote articles, a book, and even a play.

Wojtyla also spent time with students. They would go on weekend outings in the mountains to hike, bike, or ski. They also spent time canoeing on the rivers. The students called Wojtyla the Everlasting Teenager. One of Wojtyla's co-workers recalled, "When he was with young people, he seemed to relive his own student days."

Pope John Paul II hiking in Poland's Bieszczady Mountains in 1953.

In October 1962, Wojtyla was one of 2,500 council fathers the pope invited to Rome to attend the Second Vatican Council. Pope John XXIII had called the council to talk about issues that concerned the church. Wojtyla was thrilled to be a part of the historic event. The Second Vatican Council had sessions from 1962 to 1965.

No one expected the young Polish bishop to contribute much to the council. Wojtyla, however, spoke up several times during the discussions. He spoke out again the following year during the second session of the Vatican Council. He urged his fellow bishops and the cardinals in attendance to give lay people a richer role in the future of the church.

Then, perhaps remembering some of the atheist communists he'd come to know back in Poland, he spoke again. He urged those at the gathering to avoid condemning people who did not believe exactly as the official Catholic Church said they should. "It is not the role of the Church to flourish its authority in the face of unbelievers," he said. "Let us avoid all moralizing and all suggestion that the Church has a monopoly on the truth." Rather than condemning atheists, he said, the Church should look for areas of agreement and work from there.

Vatican II, as the event came to be known, changed the Catholic Church in many ways. Priests began saying Mass in the native language of their people. Before this, priests had said Mass in Latin. In addition, priests turned to face the people, rather than the altar, while saying Mass.

Catholic clergy meet in St. Peter's Basilica during the Second Vatican Council.

Man on a Mission

*V*atican II also changed Wojtyla. He became a mature leader even more dedicated to the Polish people. In 1964, he was named archbishop of Krakow. People wondered if the 44-year-old man could handle such a large job. Wojtyla quickly proved that he could.

Wojtyla was concerned about the state of health care in Poland. Many Polish hospitals had been destroyed in World War II and never rebuilt. To be treated at the remaining hospitals, patients had to put their names on a long waiting list. Wojtyla started a ministry to help the sick and disabled. He also started the Family Institute to slow the rising rates of domestic violence, alcoholism, and divorce in Polish society. In addition to his duties as archbishop, Wojtyla made time each day to visit the Institute.

Meanwhile, Wojtyla faced other problems. Poland's communist government tried to stop the Catholic Church at every turn. Catholics in Poland were discriminated against in schools, the government, and the workplace. And although Poland's population was growing, the government made it difficult for Catholics to build any new churches.

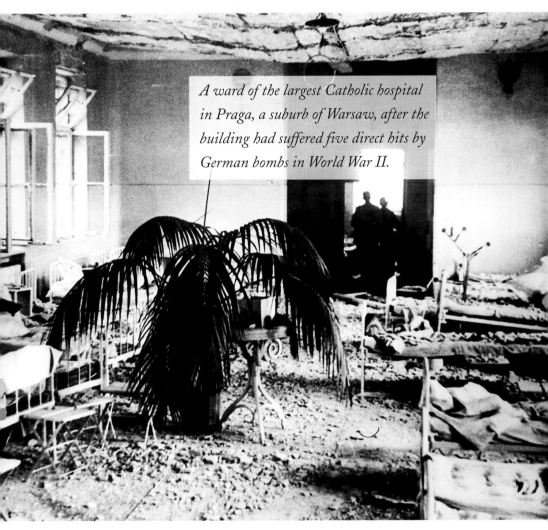

A ward of the largest Catholic hospital in Praga, a suburb of Warsaw, after the building had suffered five direct hits by German bombs in World War II.

Wojtyla fought back. He helped plan a special celebration to mark Poland's 1,000 years of Christianity. He also helped the residents of Nowa Huta, a factory town, fight for a new church. The communists had built Nowa Huta as a model city. Since the communists did not believe in God, they did not build a church in the city. After more than 20 years of protests and discussions, the people won a building permit for their church.

In 1967, Pope John VI appointed Wojtyla a cardinal. Being a cardinal is an important job, because the cardinals elect the new pope. Additionally, popes are chosen from the ranks of cardinals. As a cardinal, Wojtyla could bring even more power and respect to his job of helping the Polish people. Despite his many duties, Wojtyla still found time to escape to his beloved mountains near Krakow for hiking and skiing.

More people wanted to see Wojtyla now that he was a cardinal. He began to receive invitations to visit other nations around the world. He traveled to Australia and New Guinea. He visited France, Belgium, West Germany, and the United States.

Cardinal Karol Wojtyla

Besides traveling, Wojtyla's lifestyle changed little. Unlike many other cardinals, Wojtyla continued to wear worn, patched cassocks. If anyone bought him new clothing, he gave it away. Wojtyla also continued to have few possessions. He owned only a few books, which he used for his work.

In between traveling to other nations, Wojtyla often visited the Vatican in Rome. He was a valued contributor at the meetings there. Church officials appreciated how well he understood the situations of Catholics around the world. As a Pole, he had a special understanding for the challenges faced by Catholics who lived under communism.

By this time, Wojtyla had written many articles, essays, poems, and plays. He was known around the world as a tireless supporter for the Church and its people. And as a cardinal, he was very important in the Church. In August 1978, Wojtyla learned that Pope Paul VI had died. Wojtyla and the other cardinals traveled to Rome to elect a new pope. Italian Cardinal Albino Luciani became Pope John Paul I.

Wojtyla returned to Krakow and went to work on a new project. He worked to have the communist government lift the ban on broadcasting religious services. Little did he know that the government eventually would lift the ban, and the first broadcast would be Wojtyla's own installation as pope.

Pope John Paul I during his inaugural Mass in 1978.

A Polish Pope

*P*ope John Paul I served only 34 days as the leader of the Catholic Church. He died of a heart attack on September 28, 1978. Wojtyla and the other 110 cardinals around the world returned to Rome to select a new pope.

Once the cardinals arrive in Rome, they enter an annex of the Sistine Chapel. They take an oath to protect the secrecy of the election. Then the annex is locked, and the curtains are drawn. The next day, the cardinals attend Mass in the Sistine Chapel and begin the election process. Cardinals select a pope by casting secret ballots. A cardinal must receive at least two-thirds of the votes to become pope.

Catholics around the world waited eagerly as the selection process began. No one could say for certain who the new pope would be, but most people had their favorites. Many people believed the next pope would be Italian. There hadn't been a non-Italian pope for more than 450 years.

Cardinals file into the Sistine Chapel, where they will elect the next pope.

Inside the Sistine Chapel, the cardinals voted. At first, no cardinal received enough votes to win. The voting continued. Finally, on the eighth ballot, there was a winner—Cardinal Wojtyla of Poland! White smoke poured out of the chapel's chimney. It was the official signal to the world that a new pope had been chosen.

Wojtyla accepted his election as pope. He chose his new name to be John Paul II. Outside the chapel, St. Peter's Square was packed with people eager to hear the name of the new pope. When the announcement was made, many were puzzled. Who, they asked, was Cardinal Wojtyla? A few people in the crowd knew. They began to whisper excitedly. The world had its first Polish pope, and he was only 58 years old!

Pope John Paul II soon stepped out onto the balcony overlooking St. Peter's Square to greet the crowd. He spoke to them in perfect Italian. They responded joyfully. But the joy in St. Peter's Square could not be matched by the joy in Poland. The people couldn't believe their beloved Cardinal Wojtyla was now pope!

Pope John Paul II appears for the first time on the balcony of Saint Peter's Basilica in Vatican City.

Polish citizens hold a Solidarity banner at a rally during a visit by Pope John Paul II.

Pope John Paul II had mixed feelings about his new duties. He was thrilled to have the opportunity to serve the Church as pope. Yet now he would have to live in Rome. He would greatly miss the land and the people of Poland.

Pope John Paul II made his first trip to Poland less than eight months after becoming pope. For nine days, he traveled the country. Large, adoring crowds met him wherever he went. It was an embarrassment for the communist government. Poland was still officially atheist. Some people say the pope's visit marked the beginning of the end of communist rule in Poland.

Throughout his years as pope, John Paul II has remained close to his home country. He was a tireless supporter of the Solidarity, a freedom movement organized by Polish workers. He sent letters of encouragement to jailed Solidarity activists. The letters had to be smuggled in the folds of visiting priests' robes.

Human Rights Crusader

*P*ope John Paul II ran the Vatican with efficiency. He wasted little time on small talk at meetings. Instead, he got down to business almost immediately. Sometimes he worked 18 hours a day. He often scheduled several meetings in a single afternoon.

Part of his job as pope was to write encyclicals, which are letters to the bishops in the Catholic Church. Catholics are supposed to pay special attention to the pope's encyclicals. John Paul II's first encyclical, *Redemptor Hominis*, addressed the need for human rights. Without human rights, he wrote, societies cannot flourish.

He immediately brought his message of human rights to the world. He traveled to Mexico, Poland, and the United States. In his speeches, he criticized the unfairness and greed that kept so many people poor. He asked the governments to respect their people's basic human rights.

Pope John Paul II

Pope John Paul II greets a crowd of people at the Vatican.

When not speaking, Pope John Paul II loved to walk among the people. He preached, shook hands, and kissed babies. Every Sunday he visited parishes in Rome. He talked to the priests about local problems. He also enjoyed visiting the tombs of Italy's guardian saints.

That charming, personal touch showed the world that John Paul II was the people's pope. He preferred being out in the world to being closed up in the Vatican. Back in Rome, he scheduled weekly audiences in St. Peter's Square to move among the people. He began to ride through the crowds every week in his white jeep. People began calling it the Popemobile.

John Paul II was in the Popemobile in St. Peter's Square on May 13, 1981, when several gunshots rang out. The pope clutched his side and slid to the seat of the jeep. The jeep sped to an ambulance that was waiting at the side of St. Peter's Square. The news rippled through the crowd. The pope had been shot!

John Paul II was rushed to the hospital. He had been shot in the abdomen, arm, and hand. The bullets had passed through him, but he was bleeding heavily. Doctors spent more than five hours operating on the pope.

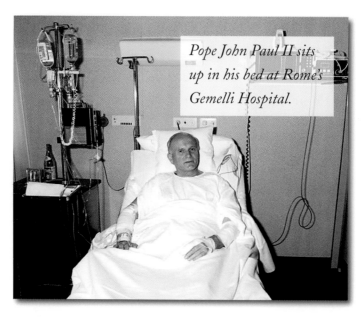

Pope John Paul II sits up in his bed at Rome's Gemelli Hospital.

In the meantime, police caught the gunman hiding in the crowd. He was a young Turkish man named Mehmet Ali Agca. Police soon learned he was wanted for murder in his homeland. A court in Rome later sentenced him to life in prison.

It took several months for the pope to recover. Almost immediately, however, the pope forgave Agca.

To this day, no one knows exactly why Agca tried to kill the pope. Some people think it was because Pope John Paul II was critical of so many governments. Whether capitalist or communist, he rebuked them for their human rights violations. He also said they were not doing enough to fight social injustice. Some people believe one or more of those governments didn't want John Paul II spreading that message.

After the attempt on his life, John Paul II had a bulletproof glass booth fitted on the Popemobile. He wouldn't be able to get quite as close to the people anymore, but the booth would offer him protection. And he would continue to speak out against injustice and abuse.

Mehmet Ali Agca, attempted assassin of Pope John Paul II, talks with the Pope at Rabibbia Jail.

Shoring Up the Church

*W*hen John Paul II became pope in 1978, the Catholic Church was at a crossroads. Vatican II had changed many of the Church's principles. It was still recovering. Some said it was floundering in a world that had outgrown it. John Paul II set out to change that.

He recalled his life in Poland. The Church was one of the few things that the Polish people could count on year after year. John Paul II believed the Catholic Church around the world needed to be that way, too. He felt the church needed to stand strong in the face of change and opposition. From his life growing up, he was used to having his church criticized. Sometimes it seemed to him that it was still that way.

As pope, John Paul II talked to Catholics about many issues. He had strict, traditional views on many matters. Thousands of Catholics disagreed with his traditional teachings. They had hoped the new pope would be more liberal.

Many Catholic leaders also disagreed with the pope. Yet John Paul II made it clear that he would not tolerate anyone within the church leadership

Pope John Paul II prays at the Cathedral Basilica of St. Louis in St. Louis, Missouri, in 1999.

disagreeing with him. He quickly disciplined any priest or bishop who disrespected his wishes. This led to further criticism. It also let other priests and bishops know what the pope expected of them. For this reason, he has been described as having an iron fist in a velvet glove.

At the same time, the pope learned to use the media and technology to his advantage. He used television, satellite transmissions, and videotapes to reach more people. An album called *Abba Pater*, which combined music with the pope praying, became an international best-seller in 1999. In 2001, the pope used the Internet to issue an official document.

Mending Fences, Seeking Peace

*T*hroughout his more than 20 years as pope, John Paul II has worked to bring people together. In May 1982, he visited Great Britain. It was the first time a pope had visited that nation. The Church of England had split off from the Roman Catholic Church more than 400 years earlier.

In 1986, John Paul II became the first pope to visit a Jewish synagogue when he prayed with Rome's chief rabbi, Elio Toaff. The pope worked to establish diplomatic relations between the Vatican and Israel. He also made a symbolic visit to Babi Yar, the scene of a Jewish massacre, while he visited Kiev, Ukraine, in 2001. Some people believe Pope John Paul II is especially sympathetic to Jews because he witnessed their persecution during World War II.

In 1989, Pope John Paul II held a meeting with Soviet leader Mikhail Gorbachev. This was a historic meeting because it was the first time a Soviet leader had been invited to the Vatican. Gorbachev's reforms later helped expand religious freedom in Soviet nations.

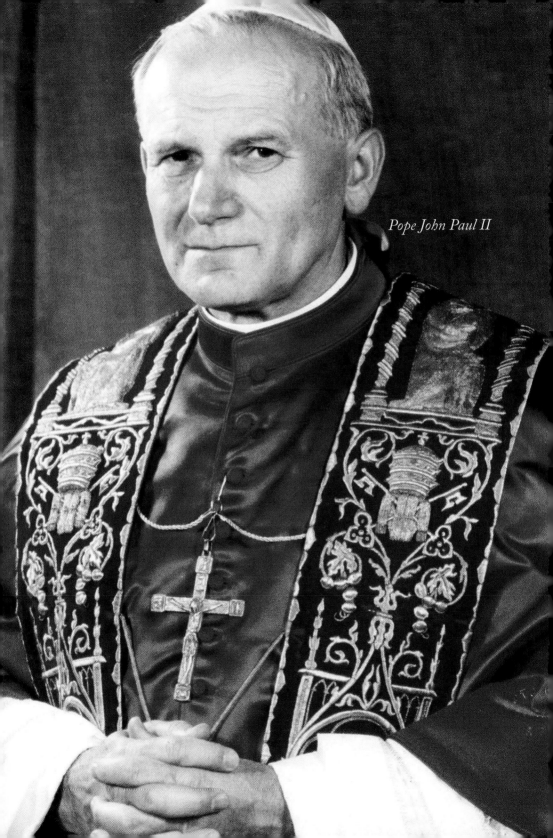

Pope John Paul II

In January 1998, Pope John Paul II visited Cuba to speak with President Fidel Castro. Communist Cuba was an atheist state until 1992 when it became a secular state. Despite this, many Cubans are Catholic. The pope urged Castro to release political prisoners who had been jailed for opposing communism. The pope encouraged Castro to permit religious freedom in Cuba. He also urged the rest of the world to open up to Cuba.

In the summer of 2001, Pope John Paul II retraced the steps of the apostle Paul. The pope's journey included a visit to Greece. While there, he asked God to forgive Catholics for sins committed against Orthodox Christians since the two churches split in 1054. The pope also has asked forgiveness for "violence that some have committed in the service of the truth." Many people believe this refers to the Inquisition and Crusades, events in which many people died.

The pope has done more than simply talk about peace. He has urged people around the world to take steps to make it happen. Part of that, he says, is not placing too much value on material things. The pope has long encouraged people to make do with less. He also has suggested that people in rich nations share more of what they have with the people of developing nations.

The pope has even said, "There is a very special, pitiable form of poverty: the poverty of selfishness, the poverty of those who will not share, of those who could be rich by giving but choose to be poor by keeping everything they have."

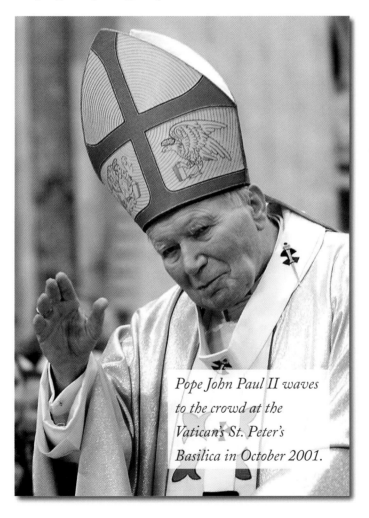

Pope John Paul II waves to the crowd at the Vatican's St. Peter's Basilica in October 2001.

A Day in the Life

*T*he pope's message of making do with less is one he lives. Pope John Paul II has never owned much. His apartment at the Vatican is furnished with few possessions. There is a single bed, two chairs, and a desk. A few icons from Poland hang on the walls.

On an average day, the pope rises at 5:30 in the morning. By 6:15, he is in his private chapel, praying. Prayer always has been an important part of Pope John Paul II's life. Friends have said the pope makes decisions "on his knees." They also credit the pope's rich prayer life for his longevity and his recovery from the surgeries he has undergone, and the wounds and illnesses he has suffered.

The pope's days are filled with prayers, meetings, and Masses. The pope also serves as bishop to Rome, so he spends time visiting the city's 320 parishes. He makes time to write and read. He also loves to participate in theological or philosophical discussions with friends and fellow religious leaders. His day often lasts until after 11:00 at night.

Pope John Paul II speaks with children in Italy.

John Paul's schedule would be difficult for anyone to maintain. The pope, however, is in his 80s. He has survived a shooting and several surgeries. He also suffers from Parkinson's Disease. Some people speculate that he may retire soon. That seems unlikely. If he did, he would be the first pope to retire in more than 700 years.

It is more likely that Pope John Paul II will continue in his mission, leading the Church in the twenty-first century. "Heaven is the time to rest," he says. "Now is the time to work."

Timeline

May 18, 1920: Karol Jozef Wojtyla is born in Wadowice, Poland.

1939: Adolf Hitler's armies attack Poland, starting World War II.

1942: Begins secretly studying for the priesthood.

1946: Is ordained as a priest in the Roman Catholic Church.

1958: Is appointed auxiliary bishop.

1964: Is appointed archbishop of Krakow.

1967: Is appointed cardinal.

1978: Is elected pope of the Roman Catholic Church.

1981: Is shot by Mehmet Ali Agca.

1986: Becomes the first pope to pray in a synagogue in the hopes of improving relations between Jews and Catholics.

1998: Travels to Cuba, urging President Fidel Castro to allow more religious freedom.

2001: Travels to Damascus, Syria, and encourages Christians and Muslims to forgive each other.

Web Sites

Would you like to learn more about Pope John Paul II?
Please visit **www.abdopub.com** to find up-to-date Web
site links about Pope John Paul II and his efforts to
strengthen the Catholic Church. These links are
routinely monitored and updated to provide the most
current information available.

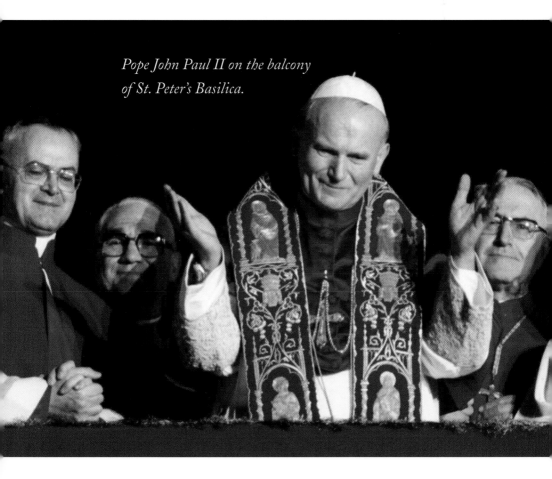

*Pope John Paul II on the balcony
of St. Peter's Basilica.*

Glossary

atheist

A person or group that does not believe in God.

cassock

A long garment worn by clergy.

communism

A social and economic system in which everything is owned by the government and given to the people as needed.

concentration camp

A place where prisoners of war and political prisoners are held.

conservative

Relating to traditional viewpoints.

diocese

The area under a bishop's control.

doctorate

One of the highest degrees given out by a university.

human rights

Rights that belong to all human beings. These rights may include freedom from unlawful imprisonment, torture, or execution.

icon

A religious image painted on a wooden panel.

infallible

Incapable of being wrong.

layman

A person who is not a member of the clergy.

Mass

The church service of the Roman Catholic Church.

parish

The area served by a particular church.

seminary

A school for training priests, ministers, or rabbis.

theology

The study of the nature of God and religious truth.

Index